IMAGES
of America

TACONY

The Quinn and Arnold families, pictured at 6804 Tulip Street in an undated photograph, were each singled out by the Disston Company in its monthly magazine *Disston Bits* as being "ideal" families in the community. In 1924, the magazine noted that two generations of the Arnold family had accumulated 256 total years at the company. Even more interesting are the families' patriotism (note the American flags), loyalty to their employer (note the central framed photograph of Henry Disston, encircled in a star), and large size. The strong ties created by multiple generations of one family working at the Disston factory helped solidify the community in its early years. As time went on, the practice of apprenticeship was forgotten, especially after the Disston family sold the company. It is interesting to note that, in 1973, Walter Arnold, descendant of the Arnolds seen above, was the last smither to retire from the Disston factory. The company resorted to placing advertisements in Sheffield, England, for skilled workers in this trade.

IMAGES
of America

TACONY

Louis M. Iatarola and Siobhán Gephart
for the Historical Society of Tacony

ARCADIA
PUBLISHING

Published by Arcadia Publishing
Charleston, South Carolina

Library of Congress Catalog Card Number: 00104061

For all general information contact Arcadia Publishing at:
Telephone 843-853-2070
Fax 843-853-0044
E-mail sales@arcadiapublishing.com
For customer service and orders:
Toll-Free 1-888-313-2665

Visit us on the Internet at www.arcadiapublishing.com

By 1683, when Thomas Holme surveyed the land for William Penn, the slightly shortened "Towaconinck" Township extended south to the Frankford Creek, including what is today Wissinoming and Mayfair. By the mid-1800s, the area had developed sporadically on the east side of the railroad and was a quiet farming, fishing, and railroad village, from whose wharf at what is now Disston Street passengers were ferried to Center City or New York. By 1898, as depicted above, the area had evolved into a thriving residential village with over 500 homes, mostly twins, whose neighboring industries east of Disston Park along the Delaware River and Pennsylvania Railroad provided the livelihood to sustain stable family lives for those who came to live in Tacony.

CONTENTS

ACKNOWLEDGMENTS

The authors and the Historical Society of Tacony would like to acknowledge the sources of the images and information conveyed in this publication. First and foremost, we would like to recognize Dr. Harry C. Silcox, whose comprehensive analysis of the Disston Saw Works and the Tacony community, titled *A Place to Live and Work*, was a valuable reference tool. With this and other publications relating to northeast Philadelphia, Dr. Silcox has brought about a renewed awareness and appreciation by today's generation of the historic significance of Tacony and nearby areas. Tina Lamb of the Tacony Library not only opened the entire library collection for our research but also submitted for our use her own postcard collection, assembled over a period of years. Her generosity and willingness to assist were greatly appreciated and demonstrated why the residents who use Tacony Library are so lucky to have her as their branch librarian.

We would like to thank Allen Wetter, the founder of the Historical Society of Tacony, for having the vision and ambition to form the organization ten years ago. Rekindling a spirit of historical awareness in Tacony seemed a tall order in 1990; this publication is a testament to the flame of Tacony pride that still burns brightly and passionately in so many of its residents. Thanks to Mr. Wetter, who also served as our "human reference book" for this publication, Tacony now has a pictorial history book it can call its own.

Very worthy of mention are the dedicated efforts of Jenny Burkhardt, who went to great lengths in retrieving little-known historical facts and memorabilia relating to Thomas W. South and the history of Tacony. We also owe a debt of gratitude to Lynn Iatarola and Jennifer Ray, who provided invaluable technical and moral support to the authors while preparing this publication. We would also like to thank Louis A. Iatarola, the president of the Historical Society of Tacony, not only for having the foresight to hire a curator (one of the authors) but also for allowing the other author, his son and employee, the latitude to balance delicately both his professional and community endeavors.

For that both he and the Historical Society of Tacony are extremely grateful.

Most important are the many people who contributed images or information for use in this book. They are Isabel Adams, Edward Barclay, Olah Bilynsky, Mr. and Mrs. Watson Bosler, Jenny Burkhart, Steven Bys, Anthony Cascarelli, Reese Cohn, Joseph and Mary Collins, Len Fairchild, Peggy Fairchild, Al Gentner, Mary R. Giberson, Harry Glenn, Marjorie Haigler, the Hamilton Disston Home and School Association, Sasha Harding, Jack Heil, Dennis Hyland and family, Louis A. Iatarola, Rev. Arthur Johnson Jr., Anna M. Keck, Barbara Eble Kelly, Benson Kessler, Thelma Koons, Virginia Kurtz, Doris Myrtle Masters, Kathryn Melsch, Joseph Morrone, Christine Nuss, Cornelius Pancoast, Angela Pody, Boots Ritter, Jeanne Roesch, Dr. Alan Rubin, Henry Rubino, Dr. Harry Silcox, Ed Sliker, James Taylor Jr., Harry Trautner, the Ullrich family, Effie Washington, Allen Wetter, Roi M. White, Harry Williams, and David Young of the Atwater Kent Museum. Information and images vital to this publication were utilized from the parish histories published by St. Vincent's (1933), Our Lady of Consolation (1967), St. Leo's (1984), Star of Hope Baptist Church (1992), and Tacony Baptist Church (1995).

Although some of the photographs submitted did not appear in the finished publication, we included as many persons as possible who gave us memorabilia to use. Our apologies to anyone we may have overlooked. We hope all who pick up this book gain some enjoyment and enlightenment from its content.

—Louis M. Iatarola and Siobhán Gephart
Tacony, Pennsylvania

INTRODUCTION

In the 1600s, present-day Tacony, or "Towacawoninck," was inhabited primarily by what had been generations of the Lenni-Lenape tribe of Native Americans. Swedish and Finnish settlers had begun to populate this wooded area along the waterfront before the arrival of William Penn. In 1683, William Penn gave orders to Henry Waldy of "Tekonay" to establish the first post office, shortening the area's name and directing Waldy "to supply passengers with horses from Philadelphia to New Castle or to the Falls." This post office, located on "Tacony Hill," northwest of the railroad, existed until 1753, when delivery by penny post began.

In 1871, seeking to escape the unhealthy conditions of his Front Street and Laurel Street factory, Henry Disston, owner of the Disston Saw Works, was attracted to Tacony for its natural setting, its transportation sources with railroad and wharf already in place, and the fact that the undeveloped area would facilitate profitable building lots for workers. He reserved 40 acres of waterfront land to move his factory to Tacony and set aside monies for streets, sewers, and a school; he visualized an ideal working-class community where workers could own or rent their own homes in close proximity to the factory. Construction of homes began c. 1875, streets were laid out in a westerly direction from the railroad, and other industries became attracted to the waterfront. Homes, mostly twins, were built with attention to light, air, and green space, which contrasted the cramped surroundings of the area near his factory. Henry Disston built a park in the center of the community to provide a natural barrier between the industries and residences. He enacted deed restrictions that would preserve a high quality of life for those who lived in the community of Tacony. These restrictions read: "No tavern or building for the sale or manufacture of Beer or Liquors of any kind or description and no court house, carpentry, blacksmith, currier or machine shop, livery stables, slaughter houses, soap or glue boiling establishment or factory of any kind whatsoever where steam-power shall be used or occupied on the said lots, tracts or piece of land or any part thereof."

These restrictions are still in full force and effect today, having been upheld by the Supreme Court of Pennsylvania in 1938, when four clubs were forced to move outside the original Disston Estate. The restrictions were upheld again in 1999 when the Superior Court of Pennsylvania upheld a previous lower court ruling that a local delicatessen could not sell alcoholic beverages based on Henry Disston's deed restrictions.

Without question, Henry Disston is the single person most responsible for the community of Tacony. The object of this publication, beyond the fascinating images it presents, is to enlighten the community about the many other people, places, and organizations (in addition to the Disstons), who have helped to make the neighborhood such a special place. Although the chapters could be interchanged, with images included in one chapter that could well have been in another, the seven categories chosen were felt to best encapsulate by theme what makes Tacony unique.

Chapters one and two ("The Neighborhood" and "People and Places") present most of the interesting streetscapes, people, and places that have been a part of the Tacony community since its days after the arrival of Henry Disston. Chapter three features what was probably the most photographed event in Tacony's history. On March 27, 1911, a fierce cyclone tore through the Philadelphia area, doing the most extensive damage in modern memory, with most devastation occurring along the Schuylkill and Delaware Rivers. As Chapter three will document, Tacony was not spared by this powerful windstorm. Few people know that Tacony was a center for technological revolution between 1890 and 1920. Chapter four ("Progress") was designed to illustrate not only Tacony's progress but also the great impact Tacony residents and manufacturers had worldwide. The Disston Company, Dodge Steel, and Gillinder Glass Works are but a sampling of Tacony's influence on the modern world.

The balance of the book focuses on the facets of Tacony that have made the community such a fine place to live for the past 130 years. Chapter five ("Pride and Patriotism") focuses on not only on the tremendous patriotism displayed by Tacony residents during the war years but also the pride in community and culture, which is so important in keeping traditions alive and neighborhoods strong.

Chapters six and seven ("Religion and Education" and "Sports and Recreation") focus on the people and institutions responsible in so many ways for Tacony's stability. The fabric of Tacony has been woven with the strongest fibers, those created through the dedication, passion, and culture of many people and places that have called Tacony home.

For the first time in a single publication, this book is a visual documentation of the rich history the neighborhood of Tacony possesses. More than 200 images have been compiled by the Historical Society of Tacony; in presenting this visual time capsule, we hope to evoke special memories for Tacony residents and introduce those unfamiliar with Tacony to this historic neighborhood.

These concrete reminders of days gone by (and some not too far gone by) are but a sampling of reasons why Tacony is such a special and unique place to live, work, play, worship, and learn. Indeed, these images show how much Tacony has changed but, at the same time, they show how much has not changed.

While preparing this book, the authors were inspired and fascinated with the many vivid stories and fond recollections these images evoked in those who were kind enough to share them with us. As much as today's Tacony can be credited to some famous and semi-famous entrepreneurs and civic leaders, most credit is owed to the thousands of residents who, throughout the community's history, have helped Tacony stay true to its founder's vision of a well-balanced, proud, working-class community.

Many hours were spent by the authors collecting and analyzing these thought-provoking images that span 116 years of Tacony history. It is our hope that these countless hours will be multiplied many times over as residents, both young and old, peruse this treasured collection of images.

One

THE NEIGHBORHOOD

In a scene worthy of a Currier and Ives lithograph, this view captures the Victorian charm of 6800–6812 Tulip Street after a substantial snowfall in the early part of the 20th century. A post office building was constructed on this block, just south of the Tacony Savings Fund Building, sometime after this photograph was taken.

The earliest records relating to land at what is now Tacony show a patent dated March 26, 1676, from Sir Edmund Andros, Swedish governor, to Michael Fredericks of 300 acres between "Pinnepakta" (now Pennypack) to "Towacawoninck," an Indian name meaning "uninhabited land" or "wilderness." The Consolidation Act of 1854, which made Tacony part of the City of Philadelphia, had a positive impact on real estate in the area. William H. Gatzmer secured the charter that made Tacony depot, as it was known by that time, the terminus for trains to and from New York. The Tacony Cottage Association heavily publicized the area in its efforts to sell building lots for the construction of St. Vincent's School and Orphanage. The area caught the attention of Henry Disston, who eventually purchased 390 acres in Tacony. When Disston purchased his tract of land at Tacony, fishing and farming quickly gave way to manufacturing. This photograph depicts the Tacony waterfront in the pre-Disston era, showing why records of William Penn's deeds in the area included privileges "of hawking, fishing and fowling."

Henry Disston was willing to grant assistance to his workers, even if advances needed to be made. Payments for workingmen's homes were made on such terms as were easiest for the buyer, including renting. A table of rents from 1887 shows a range from $7 per month for a five-room frame house to $18 per month for a nine-room brick house. This photograph depicts Hamilton (now Rawle) Street.

This is a view of Tulip Street, looking north from Tyson Avenue, c. 1887. "Tacony is a paradise for the working man . . . He can enjoy the refreshing comforts of good air, pure water and healthy surroundings. While Tacony is not what might be termed an aristocratic suburb, it has a great many handsome residences, and the pairs of pretty homes which are being erected add still more to the place." (Tacony Businessman's Association, 1907.)

MARSDEN ST. BEL. KNORR ST. TACONY PA.

Known as "Battleship" or "Gun Battery" Row, the 6700 block of Marsden Street contains the first row houses built west of Torresdale Avenue. Like "Castle Row," these homes were intended for rent or purchase by Disston employees. Marsden Street was named by the workers in honor of Jonathan Marsden, who was the first master craftsman to come to Tacony. The street got its nickname because this uniform, fortified row of homes resembled a battleship.

Disston Street, then known as Washington Avenue, is seen at its intersection with Keystone Street, prior to the time when the roadways situated perpendicular to the railroad were lowered in order to provide access east of the railroad tracks. As a result, stone retaining walls were constructed at many already elaborate Victorian-style dwellings. Note the ornate residence of Thomas W. South, on the left, without its dominant stone wall.

12

This is Knorr Street near Edmund Street in 1887. "A visit to this well ordered healthful village, a peep into the homes of the working men . . . the evident attention to light, air and other sanitary arrangements, the fair treatment which the employed has always received, these things must convince the visitor that at Tacony sure progress has been made. . . ." (Pennsylvania Secretary of Internal Affairs, 1887.)

This row of homes, known as Castle Row, is located on the 6600 block of Tulip Street, behind St. Leo's Roman Catholic Church and School. The block derived its name from the castlelike accents on the upper stories of the homes. Funds to purchase these homes were made available through a building and loan association established by the Disston firm.

This striking photograph harks back to the days before Torresdale Avenue became the main commercial thoroughfare. Looking west on Disston Street from Torresdale Avenue, this image shows the residence of John B. Moffitt on the right. Constructed *c.* 1895, the building contained 14 rooms with front, side, and rear porches. Moffitt was clerk at the Central Police Station during the 1880s and 1890s.

The Tacony Music Hall, at Longshore Avenue and Edmund Street, regularly hosted musical reviews and variety shows, often organized by owner Frank Jordan or local talent agent James J. McGowen. During the theater season, there were performances on Wednesday and Friday, with two on Saturdays. Rather than repeating a show, the visiting company would often present four different plays. Besides providing entertainment, the second-story of the hall served virtually every one of Tacony's clubs and associations.

14

Built in 1885 at Longshore Avenue and Edmund Street by local businessman Frank W. Jordan, the now historically certified Music Hall featured retail shop space on the first floor and an assembly hall on the second floor, which was used for musical performances, lodge meetings, and lectures. The third floor housed the Keystone Scientific and Literary Association. Assisted by contributions from the Disston family, the association opened the Disston Library and Free Reading Room on the third floor. This photograph was taken c. 1992, after the building had been refurbished.

This 1910 image depicts the 6800 block of Tulip Street as seen from Longshore Avenue. On the left is the Tacony Trust Fund Building; on the right is Tacony Pharmacy.

Some of the notable merchants who lined the business strip of Longshore Avenue at the beginning of the 20th century included Joseph M. Smith's Hardware Store, White and Dunker Shoe Store, J.H. Currier's Real Estate, Lister's Restaurant, Rubin Brothers' Department Store, Smithwaite Papers and Periodicals, William Boardman's Hardware Store, Gottlieb Gotthardt's Bakery, and Emma L. Stern's Millinery Shop. This photograph was taken looking west along Longshore Avenue from Keystone Street, c. 1910.

A major shift in Tacony's center occurred between 1903 and 1930. In August 1903, the No. 58 trolley was completed; it ran from Cottman Avenue to Philadelphia's Frankford section via Torresdale Avenue. Tacony laborers were now less dependent on the Disston Plant for work, and other populations entered Tacony and bolstered the labor force, increasing the community's ethnic diversity. It was during this time that Tacony's Italian population emerged.

This view of Knorr Street, c. 1910, was taken looking in a westerly direction from Edmund Street. As pre-1900 development progressed in a southerly direction, row homes began to emerge, although not as prevalent as the twin-style homes shown here. The first row homes in the area were along Rawle Street, one block east; Marsden Street, three blocks west; and at Castle Row, one block south.

This c. 1910 view of Keystone Street was taken looking in a northerly direction from Longshore Avenue. On the left was the residence of Jonathan Marsden, who built the first home west of the railroad. On the right is Disston Park, so named because it was intentionally left as open space by Henry Disston as a buffer to the industries that would employ a large percentage of Tacony.

This c. 1910 snow-covered scene looking north from Unruh Avenue depicts the 6700 block of Ditman Street. In 1887, the Commonwealth of Pennsylvania released a report compiled by the secretary of Internal Affairs that praised Tacony and Henry Disston for its harmonious and serene setting. The report was summarized by the statement, "Let the despairing go there if they wish to revive their hopes concerning the future of the working class."

"Thomas W. South is an old resident and a public spirited citizen. His fine house near the station is noticeable. I was struck with its corner miniature tower and rustic child's play-house in the rear yard, where pigeons occupy an upper story. Mr. South has done much to improve Tacony, and his battery commands the park on the glorious Fourth of July." (The Bristol Pike, 1898.) This photograph looks west on Disston Street from Keystone Street c. 1910.

18

"Every new village should begin by laying out a park, for parks have been styled the lungs of a city. A traveler cannot glance from the car window at Tacony without pleasure; let other new towns learn the lesson . . . Men are too close in dividing their land; it is easier to cover a tract with houses than to restore its natural beauty, and Philadelphia is vainly striving to regain in new parks what she has lost." (The *Bristol Pike*, 1898.)

In 1906, grocer Edward Darreff became the first merchant to follow the traffic to Torresdale Avenue after construction of the library building at Knorr Street. By 1911, 20 others had done the same. By 1930, Torresdale had almost totally replaced Longshore Avenue as the main thoroughfare. These photographs show the increase in development that accompanied the No. 58 trolley, which later became the No. 56 trolley.

"Mr. Disston and his sons have ever been mindful of all the needs, pecuniary, physical, mental, moral of their workmen and their families. They have tried to deal fairly and kindly by them; to encourage home life and good citizenship. That they have succeeded in an eminent degree cannot be questioned." (Pennsylvania Secretary of Internal Affairs, 1887.) This old photograph depicts the 7000 block of Hegerman Street.

Looking west from Torresdale Avenue, this c. 1910 image depicts Longshore Avenue. When the wave of commercial development began more than a decade later, the Tacony Office Building and modern-day post office facility were not far behind. Today, these buildings stand on the lot to the left, above, along with Sovereign Bank, formerly First Pennsylvania Bank.

In this c. 1910 photograph, looking west from Torresdale Avenue, Tyson Avenue had been developed on its south side only, with most of what was situated to the north and west being outside the Disston Estate. This photograph depicts the cast-iron Victorian lights and pairs of large twin homes that characterized Tacony at that time.

Henry Disston and his sons were renowned for having one of the first industries that exhibited environmental responsibility. This 1919 photograph shows a stand of young maple trees, which had been planted not long before by the company. The trees created a pleasant gateway to the main section of the sprawling Disston facility.

21

This 1913 image depicts a newly constructed row of homes on the 7200 block of Hegerman Street. This block became known as "Bridal Row" due to the predominant number of newlyweds who purchased new homes on this tract at the northerly end of the community.

Looking north from Knorr Street in the 1930s, this photograph depicts a bustling Torresdale Avenue business corridor. Staples on this stretch of the avenue during the mid-1900s included the Liberty Theatre, Darreff's Grocery Store, Beach's Stationery, and Them's Store.

This photograph, taken during a 1940s-era parade, depicts the 4500 block of Longshore Avenue, bounded by Ditman and Glenloch Streets. Note the vacant lot across Longshore Avenue, which is the site on which the Henry Disston School formerly stood. A row of World War II-era homes now lines the block.

This view of the 6900 block of Tulip Street was taken looking in a northerly direction from just north of Disston Street. The largest twin and single homes were typically located between Tyson and Longshore Avenues, where Disston's skilled workers began to settle in a westerly direction from the factory. That settlement began in 1875, when Jonathan Marsden constructed his residence at the northwest corner of Keystone Street and Longshore Avenue.

By the 1960s, the rows of 40-year-old mixed-use buildings had begun to feel the effect of competition from local shopping centers. Although today's Torresdale Avenue business corridor (shown c. 1977) exhibits a relatively high occupancy rate, family-owned businesses, office users, and service-oriented establishments make up most of Tacony's commercial activity. Note the old Amoco station on the right; 7-11 stands there today.

This view of Longshore Avenue looks east from Torresdale Avenue in the mid-1970s. Although over 60 years had passed since trolley tracks led Torresdale Avenue to become the commercial strip, Longshore Avenue never fully lost its commercial flavor. Robert Glassman, proprietor of Smith's Hardware (seen on the right) helped form the Tacony Business Association in 1982, which has tried to preserve the mom-and-pop flavor of the neighborhood's business district.

By the 1950s, the landscaping and circular flower bed in Disston Park, south of Disston Street, had given way to the erection of play equipment, which included a metal turtle suitable for climbing by youngsters. Eventually this section gained the nickname of "Turtle Park." After decades of use and little maintenance, what was left of Turtle Park (seen here in winter of 1994) was removed by Philadelphia's Department of Recreation in the mid-1990s.

This picturesque scene shows old-time Tacony residents enjoying a stroll through Disston Park in the spring. The backdrop of Victorian-style single-family and twin homes made the park an even finer attraction for the many passengers who could view it from the passing trains on the east.

98?? Disston Park, Tacony, Pa.

"Prominent citizens have their residences adjacent to the park. This is a feature of Tacony worthy of notice and a representation of it on canvas or through the camera would make a pretty picture. It is the first thing that attracts a visitor when leaving the (rail) cars and makes a pleasing foreground to display the fine houses that front upon it. In the spring of the year, when flowers are in bloom, the effect must be both pleasing and striking." (The *Bristol Pike*, 1898.)

Just about as old as the community itself, Magnolia Cemetery continues to be one of the most pastoral settings in Tacony. Bounded by Levick Street, Magee Avenue, and Ditman and Cottage Streets, this site sits atop what was once known as "Skeleton Hill." According to longtime resident Joseph Collins, children could sled from atop the hill at the cemetery, sometimes landing in a creek along what is now Torresdale Avenue.

Two

PEOPLE AND PLACES

Tacony Pharmacy was situated at the southwest corner of Tulip Street and Longshore Avenue, with George Whitehead, "Tacony's haberdasher," next door. The pharmacy was described in the *Tacony New Era* as "a splendidly fit-up store long regarded as the model pharmacy headquarters of Tacony." An advertisement for Whitehead's read, "New, becoming shapes in hats—exactly the same as you see shown in Chestnut Street stores, only one difference—you save 25%."

Born in 1819 in Tewkesbury, England, Henry Disston came to Philadelphia in 1833 with his father, who died three days after their arrival. Through hard work and determination, Disston started his own saw-making business in 1840, near Second and Market Streets. He eventually chose as the permanent site of his thriving business Tacony, a countrylike village that was a vacation spot for wealthy Philadelphians and home to farmers and railroad workers at the time.

Hamilton Disston (1844-1896) was the eldest son of Henry Disston and worked his way from apprentice to president of the company upon his father's death in 1878. He was at one time the largest landowner in the country, owning 6,000 square miles in Florida near where Walt Disney World is located today. His pioneering efforts paved the way for 20th-century development in central Florida.

Thomas Winfield South came to Tacony at the time of Henry Disston's 390-acre land purchase. Though never elected sheriff, a post for which he ran in 1899, South spent nearly 30 years as magistrate at the Central Police Court. He doubled as land agent for Disston-owned properties and was recognized as the single person most responsible for Tacony's growth. Upon his death, the *Philadelphia Evening Bulletin* referred to him as the "Father of Tacony."

Hon. P. E. Costello, Director of Public Work

Many of the streets and homes in the Disston Estate were constructed under the supervision of Peter E. Costello, builder and eventual Republican politician. Costello was instrumental in developing the Holmesburg, Tacony, and Frankford Railroad Company in 1901. He became 41st Ward councilman in 1894 and director of public works in 1903. He was reelected councilman in 1905, retaining that position until elected U.S. representative from the fifth district in 1922.

One of the oldest images presented in this book is this view of the residence at the southwest corner of Tulip and Disston Streets that belonged to Dr. David Umstead. Umstead delivered a large number of babies in Tacony women during the late 1800s and early 1900s. The house, which still stands today, was later expanded with a large two-story addition extending to near the Disston Street property line.

As one of the primary doctors in the area who attended to births, Dr. David Umstead kept meticulous records of the families to whom babies were born. Serving as somewhat of a micro-census, these records included not only the name and physical characteristics of the newborn but also the names of the parents, the number of siblings existing at the time, the parents' occupations, and the area from which the parents originated.

The Washington Tea House was built to serve the tastes of the predominantly English population who settled in Tacony soon after the opening of the Disston Saw Works. Henry Disston sent to his home country for skilled steelworkers for his plant; at the time, England steelworking techniques produced the purest, strongest steel. The teahouse also served coffee and doubled as a grocery store, as one can see from the signs decorating the exterior.

During the late 19th and early 20th centuries, Tacony's main street was Longshore Avenue. With a savings and loan, a department store, the Liberty Movie Theater, the police and fire stations, and the music hall (along with others), all lining a seven-block area from Torresdale Avenue to State Road, it was the commercial and cultural heart of the community. This c. 1910 photograph shows Weigleb's General Store at Longshore Avenue and Edmund Street.

This 1910 photograph of the Hirst Brothers Building at Longshore and Torresdale Avenues shows the Tacony Club in the background. It was soon apparent that Torresdale Avenue would supplant Longshore Avenue as the main commercial thoroughfare of Tacony. Later, the older structures, such as the Hirst Brothers Building, were demolished in favor of the more pedestrian-friendly row-style, mixed-use commercial establishments that line Torresdale Avenue today.

This 1913 photograph depicts John Minnich's Dry Goods and Notions Store, located at the corner of Torresdale Avenue and Knorr Street. The store advertised "New Idea Patterns, 10¢ each . . . New Idea Magazines, 5¢ each . . . our spring line of shirtings and waistings are now open, also special lines of wrappers and sateen skirts."

This photograph depicts Tacony's original police and fire station, which was situated at the southwest corner of State Road and Longshore Avenue. The building was originally constructed by Henry Disston for use as the first schoolhouse in Tacony. It was later used as the first library building, before being converted into the station building.

The Harbot Hotel was built in the Colonial style with a first-floor bar and second-floor lodging rooms. Thomas Harbot, the original proprietor, was active in political circles in Tacony, being a member of the 41st Ward Republican Club and Tacony Club, among other groups. In 1904, the *Tacony New Era* claimed Harbot "enjoys a high standing here as a thorough businessman and is one of our most reliable and progressive citizens."

Located along State Road, north of Princeton Avenue and outside the Disston Estate was Hund's Saloon, operated by Marcus and Joseph Hund from 1876 to 1890, and afterward by Hund's widow, Christina G. Hund. This establishment was heralded by the *Tacony New Era* in 1904 as "one of the most popular and liberally patronized saloons of Tacony . . . the place is handsomely fitted up with plate-glass mirrors and modern fixtures in cherry."

The Tacony Club incorporated in 1891 and met on the first floor of the Tacony Music Hall until the above building was erected in 1908 at the northeast corner of Marsden Street and Longshore Avenue. The Disston Company and a score of other associations held social events in this building. After Prohibition ended, only the Tacony Club was grandfathered and recognized by the Pennsylvania Supreme Court as an acceptable dispensary of alcoholic beverages at social events and to club members.

Lardner's Point — Tacony Pa

One of the earliest Tacony settlers was Lynford Lardner, a relative of William Penn and a landholder along the Delaware River near what is now Levick Street. Known as "Old Tacony Place," this tract featured boating docks and a stone mansion, which stood as late as 1900. This photograph shows Lardner's Point, the 20th-century name of the structure that coexisted with a city-operated waterworks and the electric light company for a time.

MERZS' HOTEL — TACONY PA

Leaders in the early days of the Tacony business community, the Merz Brothers were active in the business community and also sponsored some of Tacony's best baseball teams at the beginning of the 20th century. Their business, known as Merz's Hotel, pictured c. 1910, was located east of the Disston Estate along State Road near Knorr Street and stood where Interstate 95 is located today.

35

PENN. R. R. STATION, Tacony, Pa.

When he secured the charter for the railroad, William H. Gatzmer was president of the Camden and Amboy Railroad Company, known by the time this photograph was taken as the Philadelphia and Trenton Railroad. This station was constructed in the Victorian style prior to 1876 as one of Philadelphia's feature buildings when the city hosted the Centennial Exposition.

Pictured in 1913, the Rubin Brothers Department Store at the northeast corner of Longshore Avenue and Hegerman Street was a mainstay of the commercial strip of Longshore Avenue at the end of the 19th century. One of a handful of businesses in Tacony owned by a Jewish family, Rubin Brothers was noted for reasonable prices and flexible terms, with "dry goods, clothing and shoes" being its specialties.

The elegance of the Disston Memorial Presbyterian Church is captured in this 1887 photograph. Henry Disston was a devout Presbyterian who believed strongly that religious diversity was essential for accomplishing his vision of a harmonious, well-balanced, family-oriented community. It is likely that Mary Disston was paying homage to her husband and his faith by constructing the church in such a grand, ornate style. The property in the background, situated on what is now Disston Recreation Center, was the estate known as "The Mount," which was owned by Henry C. Forrest, vice-president of the Tacony Iron and Metal Company and the Tacony Wire Glass Company. It is no surprise that Forrest lived a short block from the president of that company and the inventor of wire glass, Frank Shuman. The building's yellow exterior, densely landscaped grounds, and high elevation made the Forrest property an attractive feature of this newer section of the neighborhood.

In 1904, construction began on a new water-pumping station and filtration plant to be located at Lardner's Point. Made to look more like an ornate public building than a utility provider, this facility was constructed in Tacony due to the influence of men like Jacob Disston, Peter E. Costello, and Thomas W. South. This *c.* 1920 photograph shows what is still known as Lardner's Point Pumping Station.

The Rubino family poses outside the family bakery, *c.* 1936, at Wellington Street and State Road. The bakery was owned by Enrico Rubino, far left, and later by his son Louis Rubino, far right. The baby is Henry Rubino (grandson to Enrico Rubino), now the owner of Rubino's Pharmacy, the oldest continuously owned family pharmacy in Philadelphia. Seated is Harry Rubino, with Guido Rubino next to him.

Andrew Fairchild, one of five brothers raised at St. Vincent's, died suddenly at the age of nine on July 27, 1932. On a picnic outing in Langhorne, the boy was found submerged in water while frolicking with other youngsters in a shallow lake, 2 feet in depth. Although Fathers Schramm and Roth tried for over an hour to revive him, while the other boys solemnly prayed, they were unsuccessful.

Carmela Fardone, nee Pellechia, is pictured outside her home at Tulip and Friendship Streets in the 1930s. At one time, she had her own hairdressing studio in the front of the house. That section was later converted to an efficiency apartment; the apartment became a traditional residence for newlyweds in the family and occasionally for single members as well. Carmela's father, Pasquale Pellechia, was born in Italy; her mother, Mary, born in the United States, lived to be 100 years old.

Four generations of the Barclay family get together in 1946 to celebrate the 80th birthday of Hester Barclay (nee Thomas), seated on the couch, third from the left. Family tradition says that the Barclay clan is the second oldest family in Tacony. Hester and Robert Barclay were the first generation, having moved from Camden, New Jersey, c. 1878. Her relatives came to the United States from Canada; he was an important man in the community for, among other things, building the Tacony Methodist Church at Longshore Avenue and Hegerman Street. A room in the church was dedicated in his honor to thank him for the contribution he made to the congregation.

Robert Barclay sits on his porch in the 1930s. At one point, an area newspaper labeled him "the most popular man in Tacony." According to the article, he was presented with a "visitors' book" on Good Friday (the year is unknown) and by Good Friday the following year, he had welcomed a total of 2,476 visitors to his home. The article stated, "Mr. Barclay is well known in many churches and hospitals for his good work" and cited especially for his work with children.

The Jacob Hepp family pose outside their home on the 4600 block of Unruh Street. This photograph was featured in the *Disston Bits*, presenting the Hepps as another ideal Tacony family, particularly for their large size. The members of the family, from left to right, are Jerry, Anthony, Mary, Lawrence, Mary Theresa holding Mildred, Raymond, Anna, Jacob, and Newman.

By the late 1930s, the Hamilton Disston School had supplanted both the Henry Disston and Mary Disston Schools as Tacony's public elementary school. The William D. Oxley American Legion Post occupied the building until it eventually moved out of the Disston Estate, having been barred from dispensing alcohol in 1938. In 1958, the St. Josaphat Ukrainian Catholic School gave new life to this building, shown in the 1940s.

This view shows the inside of DeNucci's Store, located at the northwest corner of Princeton Avenue and Tulip Street. This spot was a local favorite for "just hanging out," especially for children who attended Our Lady of Consolation School. Fr. James Rosica, pastor of the church, was known to have personally gone to the store after 9:00 p.m. on school nights to remind his students that it was probably time to go home.

This photograph of the northeast corner of Frankford Avenue and Disston Street, at the westerly periphery of Tacony, depicts a building now known as the Mannal Funeral Home. Although most of Tacony west of the Disston Estate was open space, handsome single residences dotted Disston Street as far west as Frankford Avenue. Today, most of these well-preserved structures evoke images of a time when the area was more "suburb" than "city."

Longshore Avenue remained the focal point of commercial activity in Tacony until after the installation of the cobblestone-set trolley tracks along Torresdale Avenue. By the 1920s, Torresdale Avenue was recognized as the town's commercial center, although Longshore Avenue never fully lost its commercial character. This photograph depicts Crane's Restaurant, just west of the Tacony Music Hall on Longshore Avenue.

This bakery was located at 4600 Longshore Avenue; it later moved to the 6900 block of Torresdale Avenue. The man behind the counter is presumed to be M. Hornberger, the owner; the others present are unknown. Note the Tastykakes being sold along the back of the store and the sign above them, with the slogan "The Cake That Made Mother Stop Baking."

Seen here during the "Disston School Bomber" campaign, the auditorium at Hamilton Disston School has a unique history. Jane Marsden Dixon, a fifth-grade teacher at the three Disston Schools before her retirement in 1935, donated the murals in the auditorium, one of which is on the wall at the right. She paid Philadelphia artist and children's author Carolyn Hayward to paint the murals, using images of Christopher Columbus and Hiawatha to represent exploration and discovery.

Being the only property within the Disston Estate allowed to dispense alcoholic beverages, this building became the town's center after the decline of the Tacony Music Hall during the Depression. The photograph depicts the club's 50th anniversary banquet, held in 1937. Other events at this location include a ladies' night banquet in 1940. The advertisement read, "Don't be a banquet widow—request, insist or demand that your husband or boyfriend escort you."

This photograph was dubbed by Harry Williams as "The Mayor of Philly and the Mayor of Tacony." Harry Williams, seated, made a vast number of friends during his many years in Tacony and has fond memories of the town. With him at the third annual Disston Festival on Tacony History Day, September 17, 1994, are his son Bill Williams and Edward G. Rendell, left, the mayor of Philadelphia.

By the 1930s, rows of mixed-use commercial buildings similar to those south of Tyson Avenue had sprung up between Princeton and Cottman Avenues, interspersed with detached residences and service-related properties. This gasoline pumping station and old brick "shack" was all that stood at the southeast corner of Princeton and Torresdale Avenues until Anthony Cascarelli built the present-day building as an Arco gas station in the early 1960s. Who can remember 10¢ returnable Coke bottles? or whitewall tires at 2 for $22? Cascarelli worked at this station in the 1940s and 1950s, finally purchasing it himself to erect the building that still stands and is used today strictly for automobile repairs.

Tacony native Hymen Rubin (1896-1974) graduated from Temple University Law School, established a law practice, and returned to Tacony to settle with his family. Rubin went on to serve on the board of the Tacony Trust Company and as president of Fidelity Federal Savings and Loan. He also served as president of the Tacony Merchants' Association and founded a savings and loan institute dedicated to training young men in industry.

Besides serving on the board and as president of Fidelity Federal Savings and Loan in the 1950s and 1960s, Hymen Rubin also penned more than 250 articles in the *Northeast News* called "Hi, Neighbor," in which he described events of his youth and travels throughout his life. His passion for Tacony history always shone through; he was known for displaying items of Tacony history in the bank building, pictured above in the 1980s.

This original Liberty Movie House was situated along the south side of Longshore Avenue between Hegerman and Vandike Streets. After Torresdale Avenue supplanted Longshore Avenue as the commercial strip, the theater moved to the "new" avenue. Touting the "clearest pictures in town," this building led to the decline of Tacony Music Hall, as the demand for live performance began to wane.

The original Liberty Movie House looked like this in the 1980s. Like many former commercial properties that lined Longshore Avenue at the end of the 19th century, this building was converted into a multiunit apartment building, with nearly all of its original detail either removed or concealed under aluminum siding.

Three

THE CYCLONE

This photograph, looking in a northwesterly direction from about where Tyson Avenue extends west at the left, shows a cast-iron light fixture which has been dislodged and thrown about as if it were a twig.

This view looking west along Unruh Street from State Road depicts the aftermath of the cyclone of March 27, 1911. The large stone edifice of St. Leo the Great Roman Catholic Church, visible in the background, remained unscathed by the destruction.

This view, looking south near what is now Levick Street, shows the devastation on "Gillinder Row," a row of homes in the area of Tacony known then as "Gillinderville." The homes were located in the shadow of Gillinder Glass Works.

A crowd gathered outside what was at the time the police and fire station to survey the damage. The Harbot Hotel, in existence today as Curran's Irish Inn, is shown in the background.

Looking in a southwesterly direction from near Unruh Avenue and State Road, this view shows a Holmesburg, Tacony, and Frankford Railroad Company trolley literally stopped dead in its tracks as a result of the storm. Known fondly as the "Hop, Toad, & Frog" line, this first trolley line gave Tacony greater accessibility to points north and south, as the line ran on a single track to Orthodox Street in Frankford and Rhawn Street in Holmesburg.

TACONY R.R. STATION AFTER WINDSTORM MARCH 5 2 191?

Already 35 years old at the time of the forceful storm and perched on a high elevation, the railroad station surprisingly sustained only modest damage. This photograph depicts the west side of the station.

Casper M. Titus was a "Horseshoer, Blacksmith and Wheelwright" who was active in business, social, and political circles. His father, Jacob Titus, came to Tacony in 1854 and was considered a pioneer in Tacony's early years. Before taking over his father's business, Titus was head of the blacksmithing department at the House of Corrections. Seen above, his shop along State Road was up and running one day after the windstorm.

Looking in a northerly direction, this photograph depicts State Road, the front of the Tacony Athletic Field on the right, and the trolley company's carbarn in the center. In the days before radio, billboard-style advertising was the mode of choice, as evidenced by the ads for Kolb's Bread on the left and Bull Durham cigarettes on the building in the background.

Looking east from Unruh Avenue just west of State Road toward the industries lining the Delaware River, this photograph shows the fallen power lines and support poles, which made for such a long, careful, and extensive cleanup and rehabilitation process. Some buildings never recovered and eventually required demolition.

This close-up view of the Harbot Hotel depicts the wrath to which the storm submitted this building. A hub of commercial activity in the early 1900s, the building today has been modestly restored and is in use as Curran's Irish Inn.

This view of the east side of the Pennsylvania Railroad Station shows the effect of the storm on the side that abutted Disston Park.

This photograph depicts the extensive destruction the storm caused to the trolley company's carbarn, located between State Road at the front and Tacony Street at the rear, just north of Unruh Avenue. At the time, Tacony was a single community divided into smaller neighborhoods that had names based on which industry or religious facility was in the vicinity. These included Disstonville, Gillinderville, Irishtown, and Dutchtown.

Looking south along State Road, this photograph of storm damage depicts the clubhouse and grandstands of the Tacony Athletic Field on the left with the France Packing Company building in the background at the right.

The pathway extending through Disston Park near Unruh Avenue became completely obstructed by fallen debris as a result of the storm's unusual force. Longtime residents talked about the storm's impact for years, and photographs of the devastation were used in print advertisements.

Four

PROGRESS

50 Acres

54 Buildings

3500 Employees.

HENRY DISSTON & SONS, Incorporated.
Keystone Saw, Tool, Steel and File Works   Tacony, Philadelphia, Pa.

In September 1872, Henry Disston and two other men dug part of the foundation for the first building of what was to become the largest saw manufacturing facility in the world. Having moved his expanding business from near Second and Market Streets to Front and Laurel Streets, Disston sought to establish his business away from that area's cramped surroundings. It took over 25 years to move the entire facility to Tacony.

"'The New Era' newspaper has been quite a feature in the new life of Tacony, and may it still be the New Era when the old era comes, as grown-up children are 'boys' to the mother and 'the colt' on the farm is sometimes an old horse, lovingly granted young honors." (The *Bristol Pike*, 1898.) The newspaper had its offices in what was formerly known as Tacony Hall on State Road.

In 1907, the Gillinder Glass Works, located on State Road near what is now Levick Street, employed approximately 225 people, plus 600 at its Oxford Street plant, making this company the largest manufacturer of gas and electric glassware at that time. Gillinder glass was known worldwide for its quality and craftsmanship. The company was the first to exhibit the manufacture of glass, attracting much attention at the 1876 Centennial Exposition in Philadelphia.

Another leading employer during Tacony's early development was the Erben-Harding Woolen Mill, whose mills largely manufactured knitwear and hosiery. The factory, built in 1892, was located along the waterfront, south of the Disston Saw Works. Later known as Erben, Search, and Company, it gave employment to females, as did Henry Disston and Sons.

Situated along State Road near Magee Avenue was the Tacony Iron and Metal Company. Formed in 1891 by Francis Schumann (uncle of the inventor), this company's claim to fame was having cast the William Penn Statue and decorative iron dome work that adorns the top of the Philadelphia City Hall. Teams of 16 horses hauled single pieces of the statue to the downtown location.

Delaney and Company was a glue-manufacturing facility located on the Delaware River near what is now Cottman Avenue; it was known as Township Line Road in 1907 at the time of this photograph. The plant, along with the nearby Martin Lamp-Black Works, offered unskilled labor opportunities, which allowed many Italian immigrants who settled west of the factories a chance at employment during the following decade.

The Tacony Trust Fund Building and Loan Association was formed on December 1, 1873. Shortly thereafter, this building was erected on the southeast corner of Longshore Avenue and Tulip Street. The board of directors was a virtual *Who's Who* of Tacony civic and business life, as evidenced by the officers mentioned in the *40th Anniversary Booklet* of 1913, and included Thomas W. South, John H. Currier, and Frederick Merz.

Desirable Sites for
MANUFACTORIES.
Railroad and River Facilities.

⬦ Contractor and Builder ⬦

ENGINE FOUNDATIONS,
Etc., Etc.
Correspondence Solicited.

Tacony, Philadelphia, Pa.

June 8th, 1900.

Thomas W. South Esq.,

Tacony.

Dear Sir:-

I will agree to lay a cement walk at #6743 Glenlock Street,
for a distance of 93'6", and to a width of 2'6", for the sum of Forty-two
Dollars ($42.00). The concrete base around the water closet, is not
included in this price, and will be charged for extra.

Yours very truly,

This invoice to Thomas W. South, acting as the Disston land agent, was from Peter E. Costello for the cost of improving a property on Glenloch Street with a sidewalk in 1900. South and Costello virtually oversaw the development of Tacony; Costello built many of the notable buildings, including the Frank Shuman property at Disston and Dittman Streets.

With two helpers, a Disston worker pours crucible steel in 1906. In making the best quality of steel known at the time, the English had perfected using crucibles, clay pots that have been fired. Henry Disston kept himself abreast of English steel-making processes and developed a recycling technique that quickened production and made it more cost effective. English steel was used at the plant into the 1880s.

In 1955, with some financial difficulties and waning interest on the part of the family to run the firm, Henry Disston and Sons was sold to H.K. Porter of Pittsburgh. In 1978, what was known as the Carlson Rules and Measures, Henry Disston Division of Porter Company was sold and renamed Henry Disston Division of Sandvick Saw of Sweden. This division was sold in 1984 to R.A.F. Industries and is known today as Disston Precision Incorporated.

Disston workers shear alloy metal plates, c. 1940s. The dedication of Disston's armor-plating building near Princeton Avenue and Milnor Street was one of the "last hurrahs" for Henry Disston and Sons. This plant contributed tremendously to the WW II effort, building a volume of armor plates for steel tanks; however, only ten years later, mounting cash-flow problems necessitated the sale of the company.

With a mission statement promising to manufacture the best quality steel castings that good workmanship and science can produce, the Dodge Steel Company had become a respected leader in the steel-casting industry by the late 1930s. Through the expansion of its physical facilities, which eventually amounted to over 100,000 square feet, a wider acceptance for its castings, and an accelerated shipbuilding program started in 1940, Dodge Steel's production rose from 50 tons per month in 1926 to a peak of 648 tons per month during WW II. By 1950, castings with the DS trademark were considered among the best in the world. Parts of the movie *Pride of the Marines* were filmed at the site, after Dodge Steel employee Al Schmid left the company at 21 to fight in WW II. Although blinded during a battle at Guadalcanal, Schmid singlehandedly defended his position. Of almost 1,210 Japanese soldiers who tried to cross Schmid, 18 were wounded, 2 were captured, and the rest were killed. Shown above is a 1970s aerial view of the facility.

In 1914, filmmaker "Pop" Lubin filmed a movie titled *Gods of Fate* in the vacant building that formerly housed Tacony Iron and Metal Company. During a scene that called for a fire, flames burned out of control and destroyed the whole building. On this vacant site in 1919, Kern Dodge founded the Dodge Steel Company in a 21,000 square foot building. This view shows the factory after several expansions, c. 1937.

Decreasing product demand and wage hikes, which increased from $2.83 per hour in 1970 to $8.10 per hour by the mid-1980s, led the Dodge Steel Company to close in 1986. Although a small group of the company's employees tried to save the company by taking it over from a Chicago investor, the group found itself short of capital and unable to avoid foreclosure on a substantial loan. Pictured are the factory's ruins during its 1994 demolition.

Pictured above, the *Tacony* ferry, along with the *Palmyra* ferry, provided motorists and pedestrians a means of access across a 4,800-foot span of the Delaware River. The ferries operated from 6:00 a.m. until midnight, with trips every 15 minutes. In 1922, the cost was 5¢ for a passenger trip and 45¢ for cars or trucks. In 1925, the ferries carried over 400,000 cars and trucks, over 115,000 pedestrians, and over 525,000 bus passengers.

PIO4 TACONY—PALMYRA BRIDGE OVER DELAWARE RIVER, PHILADELPHIA, PA.   2498-30

It was not until this structure was complete that the areas west and northwest of the Disston Estate became ripe for settlement. The community was no longer viewed as a suburb. Along with the Roosevelt Boulevard extension and creation of the Market-Frankford elevated line, the new bridge made access convenient from all points. The Tacony-Palmyra Bridge opened during a torrential rainstorm on August 14, 1929, with a gala ceremony, which included dignitaries and citizens.

The Tacony-Palmyra Bridge was constructed by engineer Ralph Modjeski at a cost of $5 million. It is 38 feet wide and 2,324 feet in length; 1,251,828 vehicles crossed it during its initial year of operation. The above map was produced in 1942, stressing the fact that Levick Street had become a one-way artery.

When first constructed, a one-way fare across the Tacony Palmyra Bridge was 35¢. This was reduced to 25¢ by 1952, after the span was purchased by Burlington County Bridge Commission. By 1955, the commission had paid off its purchase bonds and the fare was reduced to 5¢. By the 1970s, inflation caused an increase to 10¢; by the 1980s, the fare was 25¢. Rising maintenance and improvement costs resulted in the fare of $2 round-trip by 2000.

Frank Shuman started investigating the potential for solar energy c. 1906. He studied three previous models, improving previous designs by reflecting solar rays onto square boxes filled with ether, which has a lower boiling point than water. As a result, Shuman could power a small toy steam engine. This handbill was posted by Shuman to invite the public and potential investors to a solar energy demonstration in his yard on Disston Street.

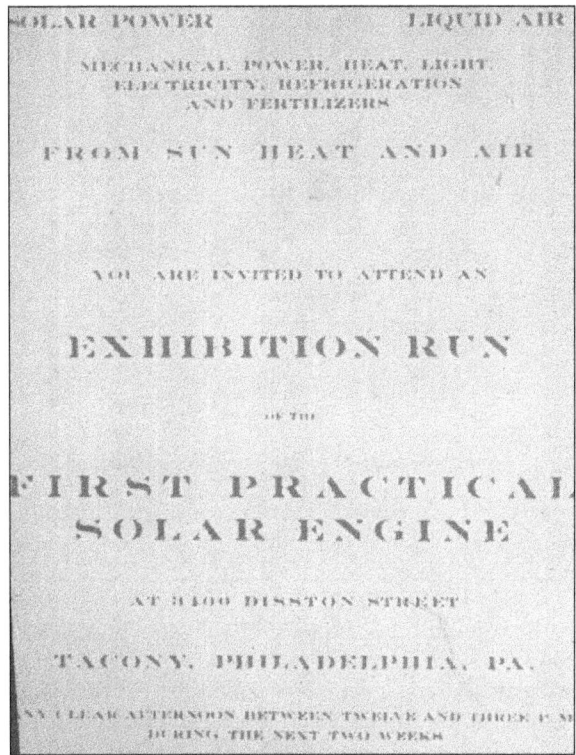

SOLAR POWER   LIQUID AIR

MECHANICAL POWER, HEAT, LIGHT,
ELECTRICITY, REFRIGERATION
AND FERTILIZERS

FROM SUN HEAT AND AIR

YOU ARE INVITED TO ATTEND AN

EXHIBITION RUN

OF THE

FIRST PRACTICAL
SOLAR ENGINE

AT 3400 DISSTON STREET

TACONY, PHILADELPHIA, PA.

ANY CLEAR AFTERNOON BETWEEN TWELVE AND THREE P. M.
DURING THE NEXT TWO WEEKS

A big reason why Tacony led the way in technological revolution was Frank Shuman, who came to Tacony in 1891 to assist his Uncle Francis with the task of creating the William Penn Statue. By that time, Shuman had owned the patent for wire glass which, at the time, was a critical invention. He was a pioneer in solar energy work and resided in this building (seen in the 1980s) at Disston and Ditman Streets.

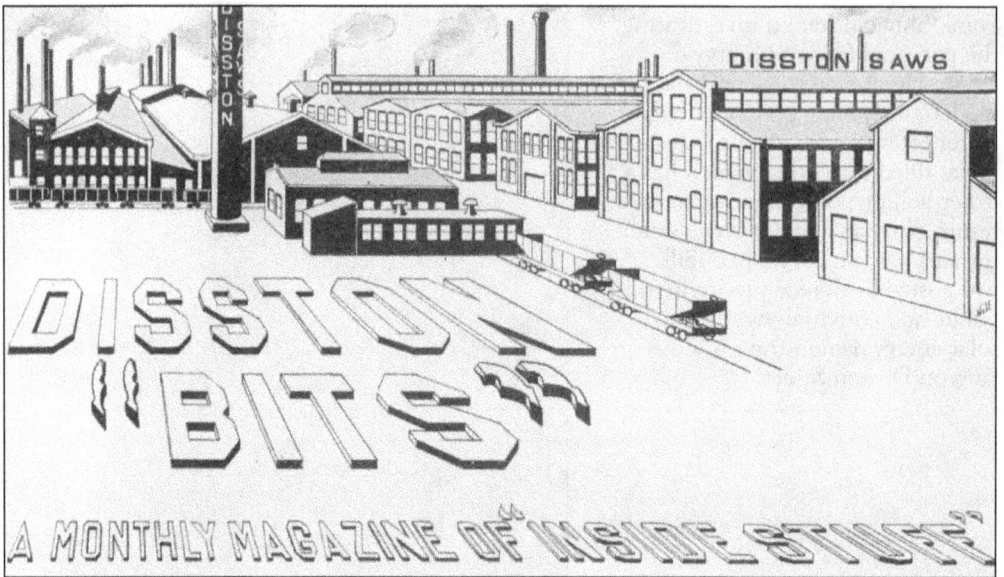

First issued in July 1917, *Disston Bits: A Monthly Magazine of "Inside Stuff"* was another example of the paternalistic outlook of the Disston family. Edited, illustrated, and published by Disston employees, the magazine was intended to solidify employee relations and maintain or enhance pride in the employer. Especially effective during WW I, the magazine featured sports and recreational activities, safety issues, and humorous cartoons.

This press conference was held to announce the new Victorian-style shelter for city-bound passengers at the Tacony Train Station in 1998. Pictured, from left to right, are a cameraman, Councilwoman Joan Krajewski, state Rep. Michael P. McGeehan, Historical Society of Tacony Pres. Louis A. Iatarola, and SEPTA Chairman Jack Leary. Krajewski and McGeehan have been very supportive in helping Tacony's civic groups with many improvement projects.

On ground donated by Jacob Disston at the southwest corner of Torresdale Avenue and Knorr Street and with building funds contributed by the Andrew Carnegie Fund, the Tacony Library opened on November 27, 1906, after outgrowing space as the Disston Library and Free Reading Room in both the Tacony Music Hall and the Tacony Trust Fund Building. One of the first recipients of a library card was Henry Disston, grandson of the founder of Henry Disston and Sons. Opening with a stock of 7,500 books, the library had more than triple that number by the 1960s. In 1927, the rear lecture room was converted into a children's book room. In 1998, the City of Philadelphia rehabilitated the building, in the process exposing an original stained-glass skylight in the main reading room and hand-painted murals in the children's room. This photograph depicts the library in the 1940s.

In 1997, the Historical Society of Tacony "adopted" a section of Disston Park from Princeton Avenue south to Disston Street and named it in honor of an active, vibrant Tacony 16-year-old named Christa Lewis, who lost her life in a tragic incident at a carnival in Russo Park on May 3, 1996. Long underutilized and somewhat neglected, this stretch of parkland was rejuvenated with new trees, new paved walkways, a new basketball court, and planting areas. Trees and hillsides can be sponsored by individuals or in memory of an event or person with an engraved stone. Seen at the official dedication ceremony in October 1997 are, from left to right, Congressman Robert A. Borski (speaking); Laura Maurer, representing Mayor Ed Rendell; Father Pidgeon of St. Hubert High School; state Rep. Michael McGeehan; state Sen. Christine Tartaglione; District Attorney Lynne Abraham; and Commissioner of Philadelphia's Department of Recreation Michael DiBerardinis. The choir of St. Hubert's High School for Girls stands at the rear. Behind the newly planted tree at the left is the former residence of Thomas W. South.

Five

PRIDE AND PATRIOTISM

This *c.* 1900 view of the northwest corner of Torresdale Avenue and Longshore Avenue depicts one of the first commercial establishments along Torresdale Avenue, known first as Emiline Street. The display with its patriotic theme is likely in anticipation of Decoration Day, now known as Memorial Day, which featured a grand parade culminating at Magnolia Cemetery.

The Tacony United Methodist Church, seen inside its present Longshore Avenue and Hegerman Street location, was the first grantee of land within the Disston Estate, along what is now Edmund Street, in 1873, according to the official *Real Estate Sales Book*, whose records were kept at the Disston Company office. The church's Easter decorations during WW I display a unique combination of patriotism and religion.

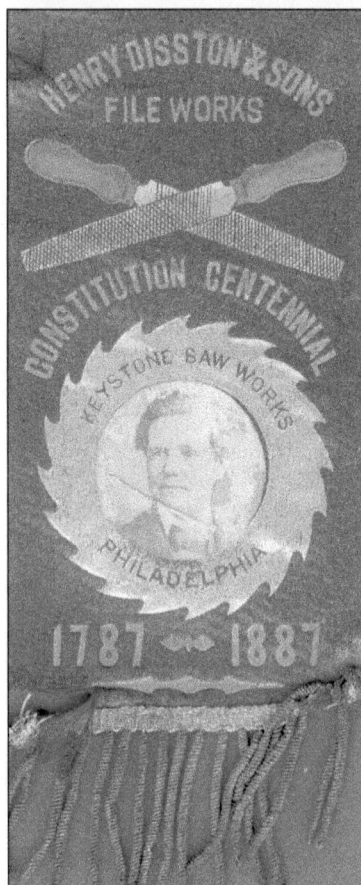

Henry Disston and Sons strove to instill pride and patriotism in its employees in many ways. For example, the company sponsored a celebration in honor of the country's 100-year centennial anniversary of the signing of the Constitution. This picture shows one of the souvenir badges from that event.

Inside photo labels: "TACONY BOYS" / "TACONY BOYS" / "TAKING OATH"

"THE DISSTON CONTINGENT OF THE NATIONAL GUARD OF PENNSYLVANIA LEAVING FOR MT. GRETNA EN ROUTE TO THE MEXICAN BORDER"

Pres. Woodrow Wilson sent troops to Mexico on two separate occasions, in 1914 and 1916, to influence the outcome of the Mexican Revolution. The Disston contingent of the National Guard of Pennsylvania was among these troops. Here, seen amidst a throng of well-wishers at the Pennsylvania Railroad Station as seen from Disston Street, the Disston employees board the train to begin their journey to the Mexican border. Whether they were part of the first or second wave of troops is unknown. Tacony became notorious for its patriotism and more than once was featured in national magazines, including *Life*. It is unlikely that any other community held as many parades with a patriotic theme during the first half of the 20th century.

This cartoon, printed in the *Disston Bits*, *c.* 1917, illustrates Taconyites fascination with both baseball and WW I. The artist imagines combining battle techniques and equipment with the national pastime. Thus, the umpire is armed and helmeted and the baseball diamond has been dug into trenches. The cartoon also shows that residents could find humor in the war, despite the many men from Tacony who were serving at the time.

This patriotic scene shows Tacony residents on the 6700 Block of Tulip Street anticipating one of the many parades that the community enjoyed during the early part of the 20th century. The war years, being especially patriotic times in our country's history, saw many parades through Tacony.

This photograph depicts the 7000 Block of Tulip Street during one of the many parades in Tacony during WW I. Seen in the background is a unique retaining wall that has semicircular grindstone halves making up the top of the wall. A portion of this wall remains today; a larger portion was removed for the construction of Our Lady of Consolation Church.

Showing patriotism while trying to raise funds for their team at the same time, members of the Liberty Boys Club parade down Torresdale Avenue in baseball uniforms during a 1919 parade. Their sign reads that they played (or practiced) at a lot near (or at) Torresdale Avenue and Princeton Avenue.

On May 24, 1919, Tacony threw a grand parade to honor those returning to Tacony and the surrounding communities from service in WW I. Some 3,500 residents and soldiers marched in that parade; it drew thousands of spectators. Girls walked before the 450 returning servicemen, spreading flower petals on the path. This scene shows the parade proceeding south along the 6600 block of Torresdale Avenue.

The above photograph depicts a WW II-era parade marching in a westerly direction by what was then the home of the William D. Oxley American Legion Post No. 133 along the 4500 Block of Longshore Avenue.

On July 4, 1943, a parade was held and a ceremony conducted at Tacony Library, pictured above. For a time, this memorial for all Tacony's war heroes was located on the lawn of the Tacony Library.

Every Memorial Day, a short parade and ceremony are held to honor Tacony's fallen heroes. This photograph depicts a modern-day winter view of the Oxley Memorial Post Monument and memorial trees. The Oxley Post has been involved in many community activities and, in the early 1990s, initiated the Operation Gateway cleanup of Disston Park and vicinity, a tradition that continues every last Saturday in April.

The above photograph looks south along the 6900 block of Torresdale Avenue during another of the popular wartime parades in the 1940s. These parades were considered an important and effective way to boost citizen's morale.

The 4700 block of Longshore Avenue can be seen during a parade in the 1950s. By the 1960s, the Vietnam War had caused some to question the importance of patriotism. As a result, large parades became a thing of the past in Tacony until the Constitution Bicentennial in 1987, when a Tacony Pride Day was sponsored by the Tacony Business Association. Since 1992, the Tacony History Day Parade has been an annual event.

1917 WORLD WAR 1918

THIS GROVE OF TREES WAS PLANTED AND
THIS TABLET IS ERECTED IN MEMORY OF OUR
COMRADES, ENLISTED FROM TACONY WHO
MADE THE SUPREME SACRIFICE IN THE SERVICE
OF THEIR COUNTRY

WILLIAM D. OXLEY

WILLIAM H. THOMPSON   HORACE W. AYRES Jr.

LEO T. McCABE

EARL W. DONALON   ALBERT W. BUCKNER

NICHOLAS CRISPI

GIACOMO MOSCARELLO   ANTHONY A. DORUSKI

EDWARD P. SMITH   JOHN J. CRONE

HAROLD B. MERZ

GEORGE W. ROBERTS Jr.   EDWARD CANTZ

HERBERT S. LYTTON

PATRICK O'BRIEN   BENJAMIN H. FISHER

MARSHALL B. LEVER

Although the William D. Oxley American Legion Post No. 133 headquarters had left Tacony by the 1950s, the post named for the first Tacony man to lose his life in WW I still plays an active role in the community and is very much part of the strong fabric of the neighborhood. In honor of all Tacony men who perished in WW I, trees were planted around a brick monument adorned by a plaque that displayed the names of the 18 men. Above is the original brass plaque that adorned the brick monument of the William D. Oxley American Legion Post No. 133 in Disston Park; it was stolen and never recovered. Each year, the post erects a similar plaque and decorates the monument beautifully during Memorial Day services.

In the ultimate show of patriotism, the students of Hamilton Disston School sold bonds and raised funds to purchase the Disston School Bomber Plane. The Treasury Rangers were the monitors of the effort to raise funds to acquire the Disston School Bomber. Posing with a caricature of Hitler and the slogan "Hang the Axis," these children took their assignment very seriously.

In addition to the school's effort to raise money for the Disston School Bomber Plane, students from Hamilton Disston School assembled in the main courtyard of the school during WW II to dismantle junk automobiles for scrap metal.

These two pictures demonstrate the manner in which students at Hamilton Disston School diligently raised funds for the Disston School Bomber during WW II. At the right, a student sells bonds door-to-door at 6912 Cottage Street. Below, students in the main hallway make changes to the signs that helped motivate students to sell war bonds.

On December 1, 1942, Henry Disston and Sons received the most prestigious award a company could receive during wartime. The Army-Navy E Pennant was presented to S. Horace Disston in recognition of the company's tremendous contribution to WW II. This pennant, emblazoned with an E for excellence, encircled in a wreath on a blue and white background, was symbolic of maximum war production and was displayed with great pride during the war years.

ARMY-NAVY

E

Presentation

TO

HENRY DISSTON & SONS
INCORPORATED

TACONY, PHILADELPHIA, PA.

★

DECEMBER 1, 1942

One of the most traditional and unique events in Tacony is the Annual Feast of the Saints Parade at Our Lady of Consolation. Since the early days of the parish, the procession of statues of various saints has taken place in the area near the church. One old-time parishioner recalled fond memories of dressing up in "Little St. Anthony" dress and following the St. Anthony statue. Above is the intersection of Edmund Street and Princeton Avenue during a procession from the 1950s.

The years 1980 and 1981 were fantastic ones for Philadelphia sports. The Phillies won the World Series, the Flyers and 76ers went to the finals, and the Eagles played in their only Super Bowl. Showing the ultimate pride in community, these enthusiastic fans pose at Tony Cascarelli's Arco Gas Station prior to their trek to New Orleans for Super Bowl XV on January 25, 1981. Tony Cascarelli is the fifth from the right.

A crowd gathers near the intersection of Longshore and Torresdale Avenues for the first annual Tacony History Day Parade on September 19, 1992. Seen in the foreground is one of several circular iron plaques that were set in the sidewalks of both Longshore and Torresdale Avenues in 1987. The plaques were designed by George Thompson and the Tacony Business Association and read, "Tacony—the Community That Bridges Yesterday with Tomorrow."

Genuine displays of pride are evidenced annually through the "porches contest" for neighbors and essay contest for the community's four elementary schools. This porch won the porches contest for the fourth annual Tacony History Day in 1996; the joint entry was submitted by the Nuss Family and Kathryn Melsch. This pair of homes is exemplary of the many pairs of well-maintained twin homes gracing Tacony today.

Near the intersection of Knorr Street and Torresdale Avenue during the third annual Tacony History Day Parade on September 17, 1994, is the Lloyd Wilson American Legion Post Drill Team from nearby Frankford. This enthusiastic group was never a disappointment when it came to livening up the festivities along the parade route.

Not only are the various military honor guards a significant and meaningful part of the annual Tacony History Day Parade; many veteran's organizations and American Legion posts are part of the festivities as well, including the William D. Oxley Post No. 133 and Tacony Memorial Post No. 735. Pictured is Vietnam Veterans Chapter No. 430 marching north on Torresdale Avenue during Tacony History Day in 1997.

Military honor guards parade down Torresdale Avenue near Tyson Avenue at the annual Tacony History Day Parade on September 18, 1999. The Tacony History Day celebrations were patterned after the Decoration Day exercises that were held with patriotic fervor a century ago. The morning parade is followed by an afternoon festival at Disston Recreation Center, featuring rides, games, and a large exhibit of historical memorabilia relating to Tacony.

Attired in traditional Ukrainian dress, students from St. Josaphat School gather before their 1999 Christmas pageant. The school has brought cultural enlightenment to the community for over 40 years, and holds concerts for the students and their families during the school year. Pictured, from left to right, are Bryant Fox, Inna Lopachuk, Darya Vselubsky, Ostap Tymchuk, Rachael Hutchinson, and Erica Carroll.

In 1998, David Young from Philadelphia's Atwater Kent Museum arranged an interesting event that was presented on the 75th anniversary of Hamilton Disston Elementary School. After a brief history presentation, he introduced William Disston and Morris Disston, who shared with the student body special and personal insights about the Disston family and their influence in Tacony. Pictured in the school auditorium, from left to right, are David Young, Principal Roberta Besden, William Disston, and Morris Disston.

Six

RELIGION AND
EDUCATION

In 1855, land was assembled by the German Roman Catholic St. Vincent's School Society
from Princeton to Cottman Avenues and the Delaware River west to the railroad tracks for the
purposes of establishing St. Vincent's Orphan Asylum and School. Between 1860 and 1879,
a three-story, double-winged building was constructed in phases and occupied a lot closer to
Princeton Avenue with the balance divided into building lots.

This graduating class from the 1930s at St. Vincent's shows, from left to right, the following: (front row) Joseph Weinsteiger, Marie Kuder, Geraldine Maier, Rev. Isadore Geist, Marie McDowell, Marie Maier, and Anthony Misch; (middle row) Joseph Fritz, John Fisher, Alex Kissimon, unidentified, Len Fairchild, and John Lynch; (back row) Dan Dwyer, Al Teubel, Fran Mueller, and Joe Pelkoffer.

The Tacony Cottage Association was formed by members of St. Vincent's Board of Managers. By 1856, sales began and gains were realized that enabled construction to start before schedule. An advertisement read: "Ye all who pay high rents in a silly corner of the city and breath pestiferous air, soon losing dollars and life, come to Tacony . . . the land is very good and the fruit of the smallest melon is much larger than that of the thickest and highest oak tree."

St. Vincent's operated a plentiful working farm. This photograph shows, from left to right, Len Fairchild, John Heiser, and Joseph Pelkoffer in the 1930s. Both boys and girls cleaned the rooms, made beds, and washed dishes daily. The girls did laundry and sewed, and the boys helped on the farm, painted the house, and maintained the roads. For 60 years, residents of the home made all of their dresses and suits.

Between 1920 and 1935, Len Fairchild and his four brothers were raised at St. Vincent's. Fairchild recalls prominently playing baseball for the St. Vincent's team and competing with rivals such as St. Leo's and Our Lady of Consolation. Pictured, from left to right, are Bill, Alvin, Emerson, and Len Fairchild.

Tacony's first church building was constructed by the Episcopal Church of the Holy Innocents in 1869 at the corner of Washington Avenue (later Disston Street) and Wissinoming Street. Consecrated by Bishop Stevens on August 22, 1872, this building was used for worship services until April 1898. Subsequently, the building was rented out for various purposes, including a school, until being sold to Star of Hope Baptist Church in 1918.

By autumn of 1873, the Tacony Methodist Church had completed this frame chapel seen in the vicinity of what is now Edmund and Disston Streets. The gradual shift of Disston employees from the Laurel Street plant increased its membership and contributions. By 1880, with the town's population rapidly expanding, Thomas South approached Rev. J.H. Moore to inform him that Edmund Street was plotted to run directly through the chapel.

90

Thomas W. South offered to exchange with Tacony Methodist Church the lot at Longshore and Hegerman Streets, and the chapel was moved to the southwest corner of the site, below Longshore Avenue on Hegerman Street. The chapel is visible at the right, dwarfed by its modern-day facility. By 1882, it was apparent that the growing population of Tacony warranted construction of a larger church building. Today's Tacony United Methodist Church was dedicated on July 5, 1883 by Bishop Andrews.

On May 12, 1884, ground was broken for the Tacony Baptist Church on a site at the northwest corner of Disston and Hegerman Streets that was given to the church by Hamilton Disston. The cornerstone was laid on June 21, 1884, and on May 21, 1885, the church was formally opened for worship. This photograph depicts the Tacony Baptist Church prior to the grindstone addition erected in 1915.

On April 22, 1882, Hamilton Disston presented the ground on which the Tacony Baptist Church now stands at Hegerman and Disston Streets. A congregation of 33 had worshiped in a frame chapel on Edmund Street near Longshore Avenue, which was subsequently converted to a feed store. This woodcut depicts the church as it appeared before any neighboring residences were built.

HENRY DISSTON MEMORIAL SCHOOL, TACONY, PA.

This building was the first public school west of Torresdale Avenue in Tacony. Appropriately named for the founder of the community, Henry Disston, and located on ground donated by the Disston family, the building was located directly across from the Mary Disston School along Longshore Avenue between Ditman and Glenloch Streets. By 1923, the building needed extensive repairs and was eventually demolished.

9815 Mary Disston School, Tacony, Pa.

As a result of the town's growing population, this building along the north side of Longshore Avenue between Ditman and Glenloch Streets was constructed to be used as the Mary Disston School of Tacony at the start of the 20th century. In the 1930s, the building became home to the Oxley American Legion Post. By 1958, the property had been purchased for use by St. Josaphat's Ukrainian Catholic Church for use as an elementary school.

The 1916 graduating class at the Mary Disston School is pictured in one of the oldest class photographs available. Most photographs of classes and sports teams were taken in front of the granite columns and stone walls that greet visitors as they approach the main entrance of the building.

The 1923 graduating class at Mary Disston School poses for a photograph that features Principal William Moran, front right, as well as five teachers, from left to right in the back row, Russell McBride, Adelaide Comly, William Flischman, Edna Whittaker, and Morrison Booth.

At the beginning of the 20th century, it became apparent that St. Leo's Parish was in need of a school facility for Tacony's rapidly growing population. By September 1908, the original school (the northernmost portion of today's facility) was opened to 221 elementary school students. Two more additions in a southerly direction were completed by 1925, as the school passed the 500 student mark. Another addition in 1953 added eight classrooms and kindergarten space on the first floor at a cost of approximately $300,000.

In 1908, St. Leo the Great Church (with its convent on the left) began with a group of non-German Catholics who resided in Tacony and wanted a parish to serve the English-speaking, mostly Irish Catholics of the town. Masses for most Tacony Catholics took place at St. Vincent's Chapel; however, the vernacular portion of the mass and various other ceremonies were conducted in German. Mary Disston had sold the archdiocese a site at Unruh Avenue and Keystone Street for construction of St. Leo's Church in 1885, only one year after Fr. Joseph Strahan, the founding pastor, had rented a house for the church. Later that year, the basement of the church and original portion of the rectory (today's convent) were built. The church was officially dedicated on November 24, 1895, at a ceremony presided over by Archbishop Patrick J. Ryan.

Father Bowen of St. Leo's School poses with the girls of the First Holy Communion class in 1928.

The above photograph depicts the Disston Memorial Presbyterian Church and Parsonage on the west. These facilities occupy an entire block of Tyson Avenue between Glenloch and Jackson Streets. The deep tones of the church's bell can still be heard on any given Sunday morning.

The Star of Hope Baptist Church dates from 1917, when African-American families from Rice, Virginia, migrated to Tacony for work at the Disston factory. The congregation eventually purchased the old Holy Innocents Church at Wissinoming and Disston Streets, which was used as a school after the original church was vacated. In May 1918, the first service was held in this building. The construction of Interstate 95 forced the congregation to seek a new home in 1959.

To promote sociability among the younger element of Catholic men in Tacony, the Hamilton Catholic Club was formed on December 5, 1901, with a meeting room on Hamilton (now Rawle) Street, from which the club got its name. Seen here, from left to right, are W. Kalblein, T. Corcoran, unidentified, A. Grant, G. McKinney, J. League, Harry Kane (the first child baptized at St. Leo's), L. Carroll, and J. Furphy.

In the years after its grindstone expansion, the Tacony Baptist Church had its own brass band, under the direction of its pastor Reverend Tryon. The Tryon Bible Class Band poses on the Disston Street side of the building; notice the construction that is the building's trademark.

By 1914, approximately 30 families from a small Italian town called Cosenza had settled in a northerly part of Tacony and sought to form an Italian Catholic Parish. By 1917, and after using the chapel at St. Vincent's, Rev. Alfredo Procopio, assistant to the pastor of Mater Dolorosa Church in Frankford, borrowed $10,000 to facilitate construction of this church, the first Our Lady of Consolation Church at Wellington and Edmund Streets.

The church bell which rests in the Bell Tower at Tacony Baptist Church was cast in 1860 and was used at a Sanitary Fair in Logan Square to raise money for the care of wounded Civil War veterans. Henry Disston purchased the bell for use at the tower of the factory, but decayed timbers forced him to store it in the yard. Church member William C. Hallman was instrumental in persuading the company to let the church place the bell in its tower on "permanent loan." Members of the Tacony Baptist Church pose outside, after the addition of the grindstone wing. They are, from left to right, as follows: (front row) unidentified, Mr. McCallah, Pastor Green, Frank Griffith, and Sleus Booze; (middle row) George Still, Mr. Glass, Mr. Cole, George ?, Eltin Udell, and Johnson Stockton; (back row): Mr. Terry, Gus Zimmerman, Walter Gill, Mr. Cronch, Walter Kay, and George Guyer.

Father Agnello Angelini, the second pastor of Our Lady of Consolation Parish, poses with the girls of the First Holy Communion Class of 1928.

Seeking to find a more serene setting away from the industry that had sprung up around their original church, Holy Innocents Episcopal Church built this elegant stone building in 1897. On Easter Sunday of 1898, the first service was held. In 1903, extensive alterations were made, including the addition of classrooms, an organ, an enlarged Sunday school room, and new stained-glass windows.

Seen from Torresdale Avenue during a Strawberry Festival in 1978, the Holy Innocents Episcopal Church has been an active part of Tacony's past. The June Strawberry Festival and September Peach Festival are much anticipated annual traditions. On November 18, 1992, this church merged with St. Paul's Episcopal Church from Aramingo Avenue to form Holy Innocents-St. Paul's Church. A large stone addition, in keeping with the original architecture, was erected in 1998.

This photographs shows Holy Innocents Episcopal Church holding its annual Strawberry Festival in 1978. Part flea market, part cookout, part strawberry-and-ice-cream-fest, but mostly a chance for neighborly conversation and reminiscing, this event has been a festive part of Tacony's history for decades.

Hamilton Disston School

Named for a unique person, a forward thinker and public servant, the Hamilton Disston School was erected in 1923 at Knorr Street between Gillespie and Cottage Streets on land donated by the Disston Family. Hamilton Disston had not only helped to carry out his father's vision of a "New" Tacony, but had also served as the fire department commissioner and the Fairmount Park commissioner. It was during his tenure as Fairmount Park commissioner that Disston Park was extended to its present southern boundary. Upon its construction, this state-of-the-art public school building was praised for its fireproof construction, "pure heated air to each classroom" and an auditorium "with motion picture booth, stage and dressing room." Seen here not long after being erected, the school has details, such as the elaborate stained-glass set-in arched windows, that today are prominent reminders of the craftsmanship of a bygone era.

This photograph depicts the first graduating class of Hamilton Disston Elementary School. The building was constructed in 1923 with a seating capacity of 1,500 pupils at a cost of $547,453. The image dates from 1925.

In outfits reminiscent of half a century ago, the school safety patrol poses along the Gillespie Street side of Hamilton Disston School in the early 1950s. Would there be safeties in today's elementary schools if they were made to wear such uniforms?

M. DAMIS · M. CALLUM · M. CREUTZINGER · L. FEHR · F. ROSE · E. KUEHNLE · T. HULME · C. FRANKENHAUS

J. AFFATATO · R. DIEROLF · C. LUNT · B. ZICCARDI · V. KERSHNER · T. SULLIVAN · M. BERGMEISTER · O. RUOFF

N. AMOROSO · H. WHITTLE · T. GRAHAM · R. LUCERA · G. LEVY · D. MCKINLEY

M. PITTMAN · D. GRAFF · A. CATALANO · L. MCCULLOUGH · M. REDDICK · W. BAEDER

R. Kurtz Vice Pres.

K. THOMPSON · D. KIDD · B. THOMPSON · G. HANAFY · G. MASON · R. VOLLMER

JUNE

E. MALATESTA · J. SOMERVILLE · E. PUDDY · G. VERNON · D. KLEIN · J. PRELLE · S. SCHEIBLEIN · J. Seife

This image is one of the more unique graduating class photographs of Hamilton Disston School. Instead of a group shot, it features individual photographs and the names of all graduates. The original framed copy, on display at the Historical Society of Tacony office, contains original signatures of most graduates (and some teachers) on the back of the photograph. The students who attended this fine elementary school at that time were fortunate to have the "largest

104

...Y	S. CLARK	F. TRIGIANI	E. LOUCKS	J. MURPHY	E. WARRINGTON	C. HOFFMANN	I. O'BRIEN	W. PRENDER...

...D | W. WOLFE | D. MUSSELMAN | W. NUSS | M. MATTOX | J. REINHART | T. MALEY | C. WERNES | M. MAPLE...

TON

J. INGRAM | F. YOUNG | C. PARAVICINI | R. USLIN | I. SHIFFLETT | J. CONLAN...

R. DOWNING | M. SHANNON | A. RENNIE | C. MENDITTO | W. CLIFT | M. HICKMA...

H. Morris Pres.

1940

ncipal.

R. COOK | H. BOWERS | B. CREEDON | L. CLYNES | R. DOUGHERTY | J. LAURO

...ckett, Secy.

J. KIEFER | G. LUTZ | K. TYLER | J. MOSCATO | M. LOSE | J. DEFINIS | C. EMERY

elementary Home and School Association in the United States," as proclaimed in newsletters from 1939. The association sponsored cultural events, such as theatrical shows and dances, as well as important discussions on topics such as "Government and Education." Welcomed to that discussion on January 18, 1937, were mothers interested in finding out "from experts how our schools are run in Pennsylvania."

The Tacony Presbyterian Church began a Sunday School in 1883, with activities conducted at Tacony Hall. The school prospered, and Mary Disston chose to erect and donate to the congregation this magnificent structure, now known as Disston Memorial Presbyterian Church. Dedicated in memory of her husband, Henry Disston, and their daughter who died at a young age, the church was situated at the southwest corner of Glenloch Street and Tyson Avenue.

In July 1890, German Lutheran families in Tacony opened a Sunday school. A church organization was formed shortly thereafter and held its first worship service at the Tacony Music Hall. By the mid-1890s, the church building, seen here c. 1910, and still in active use today as St. Petri's Lutheran Church, stood like a beacon in the midst of what was primarily open space at the time.

Temple Menorah was dedicated on November 9, 1952, to serve the fast-growing congregation of the Northeast Jewish Community Center. Renamed because of the large menorahs at the entrance, the new building was adorned with stained-glass panel windows at the side and three Mogen David stars at the roofline. This building includes a stage, a kitchen, classrooms, and an auditorium named after its founder, Miriam Magil Rubin. The congregation is now known as Temple Menorah Keneseth Chai.

Miriam Magil Rubin (1898–1977), wife of Hymen Rubin, founded the Tacony Women's Hebrew Association on the second floor of the Tacony Savings Fund Building in 1925. In search of a learning and worship center for the children of approximately 25 Jewish families who had settled in Tacony, the congregation eventually formed in an old Acme Store at Tyson Avenue and Walker Street in 1936. They called themselves the Northeast Jewish Community Center.

Known as the Shul, this building served as the home of the Northeast Jewish Community Center from 1936 to 1952. The main synagogue was in the center of the building, with makeshift classrooms along the sides and in the basement. Adorned modestly by the letters "NJCC" within a Mogen David star at the front and a Jewish star set in stained-glass, the building could hold about 100 members.

This residence that once stood at 7049–7051 Tulip Street is now the site of Our Lady of Consolation Church. In 1955, after residing there for less than seven years, Constance (Mabel) Giovannelli and her husband Orlando were approached by Rev. James V. Rosica about purchasing the property for construction of a new church building. Without hesitation, the Giovannellis agreed and, by year's end, ground was broken for the modern-day facility.

Rev. James V. Rosica receives the keys to the property at 7049–7051 Tulip Street for the construction of Our Lady of Consolation Church. With Father Rosica in this ceremonial photograph are, from left to right, Constance (Mabel) Giovannelli, Orlando Giovannelli, and Anthony Giovannelli.

On December 21, 1956, Arch. John J. O'Hara dedicated the new church of Our Lady of Consolation Parish with a solemn pontifical mass celebrated by the most Rev. Joseph M. McShea, auxiliary bishop of Philadelphia. Designed by Philadelphia architects John Sabatino and Morton Fishman, the building features a granite entryway dominated by a white marble statue of Our Lady of Consolation.

In February 1928, ground was broken at the southeast corner of Princeton Avenue and Edmund Street for a combination church and parochial school building to serve the growing Italian parish of Our Lady of Consolation. By October of that year, the new church-school facility was dedicated by Bishop Michael Crane. Upon the construction of the modern-day church on Tulip Street, this building was renovated into a classroom building at a cost of approximately $100,000 in 1958, with a rectory added at the southwest corner of Tulip Street and Princeton Avenue in 1960. Rev. James V. Rosica, the pastor of the church at the time, came to the parish as a 26-year-old priest in 1933 and was credited largely for lifting the parish out of postdepression debt and bringing the parishioner total to 1,350 families by 1967.

After being notified that their church building at the corner of Disston Street and Wissinoming Street had to be demolished for the construction of Interstate 95, members of the Star of Hope Baptist Church purchased a parcel of ground at the northeast corner of Friendship and Hegerman Streets for their permanent home. This fine brick building was constructed in 1962 and has since been accompanied by an annex building across Friendship Street.

This is an interior view of the lovely sanctuary at the 40-year-old Star of Hope Baptist Church. The congregation has been actively involved with various service and religious activities and its Pioneer Club, comprised of the youth of the church, has been active in Tacony History Day Festivities.

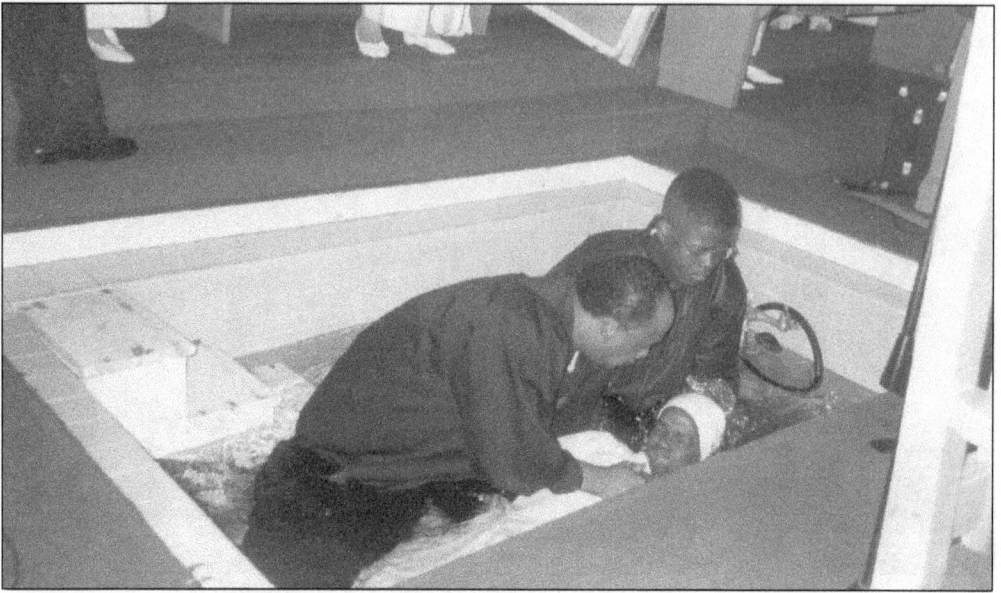

A special moment for the Star of Hope Baptist Church community occurs as a member is taken into the fullest experience of her faith through baptism. Rev. Melvin Williams, left, and Rev. George Nelson, right, baptize Ashley Blackmon.

These happy children are the members of the Star of Hope Baptist Church's Pioneer Club in 1989. The Pioneer Club is a national Christian service organization. Star of Hope's chapter began in 1987. Service activities include supporting three shelters, donating clothing and toys, and visiting those who are sick or homebound. Effie Washington, front left, has been the group's coordinator since it began.

This brick building with its one-story extension is the home of St. Stephen's United Church of Christ, which is situated at the northeast corner of Princeton Avenue and Erdrick Street. The congregation has been holding Sunday worship services at this facility since 1949.

This building, situated at the southeast corner of Tyson Avenue and Vandike Street, is home to Pentecostal Christian Church. The congregation dates back to 1926; the building was erected in 1960. This church serves a mostly Italian Protestant congregation.

Good Shepherd Church began at Tyson Avenue and Walker Street in a vacant store that became the home of the first Tacony synagogue. On September 16, 1928, the first worship service was held there and, by 1929, the Evangelical Lutheran Church of the Good Shepherd had 103 members. A lot was purchased at Erdrick Street and Cottman Avenue in 1930. Today's facility, pictured above, was constructed in 1957, after the original chapel was outgrown.

Arriving at Tacony Baptist Church c. 1980, Pastor Arthur Johnson Jr. breathed new life into this old church. He not only strengthened its dwindling congregation through his passionate preaching, but also, with his friendly demeanor and unflappable enthusiasm, endeared himself to nearly everyone who has crossed his path. Active in many organizations, he also started a food bank that has provided a real boost to those in need.

114

This recent photograph of the Tacony Baptist Church depicts its trademark grindstone construction. These grindstones, weathered from having been discarded and stored in the yard at Henry Disston and Sons, were broken, squared, trimmed, and used as the facade of the 1915 addition, hence, the church's nickname as the "Grindstone Church."

On the Disston Street side of the school, St. Josaphat School students pay homage to Mary during the annual May Procession in 1998. Seen in the background, the brick addition to the original stone building, which was the Mary Disston School, features an elevated walkway leading to a large auditorium with a basketball court, a kitchen, a library, and classroom facilities.

In December 1953, the Hamilton Disston School was paid a visit by the "Jolly Old Elf" himself, Santa Claus, as depicted above from a supplement of its school newspaper, known as the *Disston Keystone*.

Adding a meaningful touch to the holiday season by celebrating the diversity of Christmas around the world, St. Josaphat School students are shown in a multitude of styles of traditional holiday dress on stage in the school auditorium during the 1995 Christmas pageant.

Seven

SPORTS AND
RECREATION

The baseball team of the Mary Disston School poses for this 1918 photograph. The popularity of baseball in Tacony came to an all-time high in 1918, after waning a bit in the early years of the 20th century, as the popularity of soccer grew.

KEYSTONE COURSE.

ENTERTAINMENT
—IN—
TACONY HALL, TACONY,
—ON—
TUESDAY EVENING, APRIL 22d, 1879,
—BY THE—
Keystone Scientific and Literary Association Members.

"HOW HE SAVED ST. MICHAEL'S,"
MISS ANNIE GLENN.

"TOO LATE FOR THE TRAIN,"
WILLIAM MILLER.

"EVIL SPEAKING," (Original.)
MRS. T. W. WORRELL.

"DEATH BED OF BENEDICT ARNOLD."
J. H. HULSE.

"WOMAN IN BUSINESS." (Original.)
MRS. M. LOUISE THOMAS.

DISCUSSION.
REV. C. H. KIDDER, OMAR J. KINSLEY, AND OTHERS.

MUSICAL DIRECTOR---MR T. WORCESTER WORRELL.

Tickets, - 20 Cents.

To be procured at Frederick C. Orth's Drug Store, Holmesburg,
and O. J. Kinsley's, Mrs. Mills' and J. H. Currier's stores, in Tacony.
The tickets on sale in Holmesburg are 35 cents each, including reserved seat and transportation to and from the Hall.
Stage leaves from front of F. C. Orth's Drug Store, Holmesburg
at 7.15, sharp.
Doors open at 7 o'clock - To commence at 7.45 o'clock.

Wm. F. Knott, Printer, Frankford.

Cultural entertainment flourished in Tacony during the 1870s and 1880s. Tacony Hall and the Music Hall provided two venues for musical and spoken recitals. This handbill advertises a performance by members of the Keystone Scientific and Literary Association. Tickets were 20¢, while 15¢ more could purchase a round-trip via stagecoach from Orth's Drugstore in Holmesburg. The association sponsored topics and guest speakers, such as Susan B. Anthony (suffrage) and P.T. Barnum (temperance).

In the early 1900s, young Bill Arnold proudly displayed the animal skins and rifle used in his successful quest at the rear of his family's residence at 6804 Tulip Street.

In this whimsical pose from the early 1900s, these Tacony residents take aim at several members of the abundant rabbit population of Tacony. Demonstrating one of the more primitive pastimes in the old days of the community are members of the Arnold family at the rear of 6804 Tulip Street. The fate of the rabbits was never discovered.

Although unable to identify either where this scene is or the individuals in it, the Forrest Club was a group of men and women from Tacony. Judging from their attire, it is likely that the club was comprised of a group of local actors and was named after prominent actor Edwin Forrest, a Philadelphian whose estate was located in Holmesburg, on grounds now occupied by the Forrest Elementary School.

This photograph depicts the St. Leo's Players, a theatrical group based at St. Leo's Parish. This 1923 photograph, with Rev. William Gaughan, is from a St. Patrick's Day production titled *Arah A Pogh*.

Mule rides, with the option of a photograph, were a popular form of recreation in the first part of the 20th century. Pictured in 1923 are 5-year-old Harry Williams and his sister Margery Williams in front of their home at 6621 Tulip Street. Both children were born in the front bedroom of 6619 Tulip Street. One of Harry Willliams's greatest memories was standing on the Tacony Palmyra Bridge during its official opening.

The first Tacony baseball team was formed by F.B. Fisher in 1889. The team's uniforms were described years later as "the loud red suits." The red shirts, black stockings, red pants, white belts, and red-and-white hats were said to make quite an impression on the field. Grouped in front of manager J. Fisher, rear, are, from left to right, the following: (front row) ? Bergen and ? Glenn; (middle row), ? McFadden, ? Gardner, B. Brown, and B. Wright; (back row) Al Butterworth, H. Baker, M. Ploucher, ? Kelly, and Pop Faldon. (*Disston Bits.*)

Pitcher Billy Seeds became a hero in Tacony when he joined the Boston Red Sox in the 1890s. Tacony remained his home, where his nickname was "Sox." The members of this early Tacony team, from left to right, are as follows: (front row) Dan Bergen and Jack Glenn; (middle row) Bobby Brown, Dinky Gardner, manager John Fisher, Joe McElhaugh, and Billy Seeds; (back row) Bert Wright, Mace Ploucher, and Herb Baker. (*Disston Bits.*)

Tacony's first soccer team was organized in 1891. According to the *Disston Bits*, the team generally won all it games, except in Trenton, where it had a difficult time beating the Potters on home turf. Pictured, from left to right, are the following: (front row) J. Lister, B. Adams, J. McGurk, J. Ervin, and T. Moore; (second row) H. Williamson, J. Stewart, S. Needham, and M. West; (third row) B. Graves, H. Crowhurst, J. Edgar, and J. Greenhouse; (fourth row) J. Elias, J. Gamble, W. Tuas, and W. Broomhead.

This postcard from early in the 20th century is titled "Young Tacony out for Great Sport." It depicts exuberant children out for a sledding excursion at Disston Park. They are gathered at what is now the entrance to the Christa Lewis Memorial Arboretum. This elevated park still serves as a popular sledding spot for the youth of Tacony.

Henry Disston encouraged all his workers, including the women, to get involved in sports. At lunchtime, women employed in the office would play dodge ball. In 1919, women's baseball and track teams were formed. Pictured is the 1919 baseball team, from left to right, as follows: (front row) Gertrude Terry, Kathryn Hennessey, Dorothy Musgrave, and Anna Checchia; (back row) Lillian Austin, Ella Kruse, Beryl Newman, and Helen Sanford. Another player, Marie Lester, is not in this picture.

This photograph shows the St. Leo's Football Team of 1927. By that time, baseball, soccer, football, and basketball had become a part of many of the lives of Tacony's youth.

During the first half of the 20th century, the Tacony Public Bath House was a popular swimming spot for young and old alike. Lovingly dubbed the "Bathie" by many residents, who recall the structure, the building was located near the Tacony-Palmyra Bridge in the southeast corner of the neighborhood.

In this c. 1940s photograph, lifelong Tacony resident Kathryn Boardman Melsch poses before jumping in to take a swim at the Tacony Public Bath House. She was a niece of the proprietors of Boardman's House Furnishings Store, a staple of old Longshore Avenue between Tulip and Edmund Streets. Her husband was a longtime Disston employee. She passed away in 1999.

By 1942, organized sports for girls were commonplace in Tacony, as evidenced by this photograph depicting the girls' basketball team from St. Leo's.

This photograph depicts the Tacony Aces football team, which had its clubhouse (also serving as equipment storage building) in a garage along Unruh Avenue between Hegerman and Edmund Streets. A local tradition in the early part of the 20th century was a Thanksgiving Day game between the Aces and St. Leo's football team.

The football team of Tacony Boys Club was photographed in 1946. Throughout its history, Tacony has benefited from the commitment of local business and civic leaders who have served as sponsors and as coaches. This tradition continues today. People, such as Joseph McCloskey, who lent countless hours coaching with Tacony's team of the Police Athletic League up to the 1970s, had a profound impact on those who coach Tacony's youth of today.

Equipped with musical instruments in the courtyard of Hamilton Disston School, the school;s Music Club poses for this 1952 photograph. The Disston Orchestra was widely respected and hailed by a local newspaper in 1936 as "outstanding among school or junior orchestras." At that time, William Metzner was the conductor.

126

Hamilton Disston School's Home and School Association had a very active Plays and Players acting group in the 1950s. The above photograph depicts its production of *Tune In*, a musical comedy in two acts about a fictional television station known as WTNT. The shows was presented on April 28 and April 29, 1955. Helen Soehle is the trainer, and Al Nicol and Al Gorman are the front and back of the horse.

Near the center of the action of Tacony's new Torresdale Avenue commercial corridor was the "new" Liberty Movie Theater, with its trademark painted shieldlike emblems flanking a series of entry doors at the front. The building was Tacony's neighborhood movie theater until the 1960s, when changing leisure patterns gave way to construction of multiplex style theaters.

This photograph shows the decorative interior of the Liberty Theatre as it appeared during its heyday. After the movie theater closed in the 1960s, the building was used as a catering hall (appropriately named Liberty Caterers). Later known as Golden Eagle Caterers, the building hosted events ranging from political fund-raisers to wrestling matches. Today, the building is used as Body-Tech Fitness Center.

The Disston Recreation Center was built in 1931, and its fields occupy two square blocks at Glenloch and Disston Streets. This centrally located building has served a wide variety of Tacony's recreational needs. In the 1980s, the building was in need of repairs and in danger of closing when Councilwoman Joan Krajewski secured funding for repairs and renovations. Today, the building bustles with daily sports activity and is host to many special events.

Visit us at
arcadiapublishing.com

www.ingramcontent.com/pod-product-compliance
Lightning Source LLC
Chambersburg PA
CBHW080909100426
42812CB00007B/2215